HAL•LEONARD
ESSENTIAL SONGS

PIANO VOCAL GUITAR

Christmas

CO-AUR-631

ISBN 0-634-08900-5

HAL•LEONARD®
CORPORATION
7777 W. BLUEMOUND RD. P.O. BOX 13819 MILWAUKEE, WI 53213

Visit Hal Leonard Online at
www.halleonard.com

CONTENTS

A CAROLING WE GO

Music and Lyrics by
JOHNNY MARKS

ALMOST DAY

Words and Music by
HUDDIE LEDBETTER

AS LONG AS THERE'S CHRISTMAS

from Walt Disney's BEAUTY AND THE BEAST - THE ENCHANTED CHRISTMAS

Music by RACHEL PORTMAN
Lyrics by DON BLACK

Tempo I

AWAY IN A MANGER

Traditional
Words by JOHN T. McFARLAND (v.3)
Music by JAMES R. MURRAY

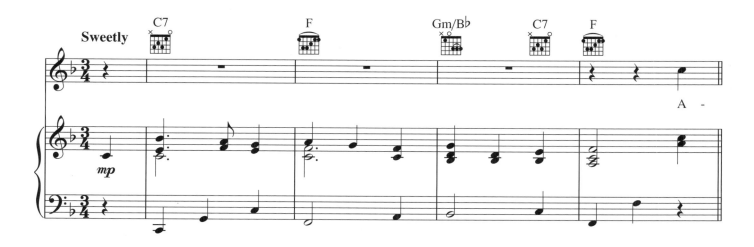

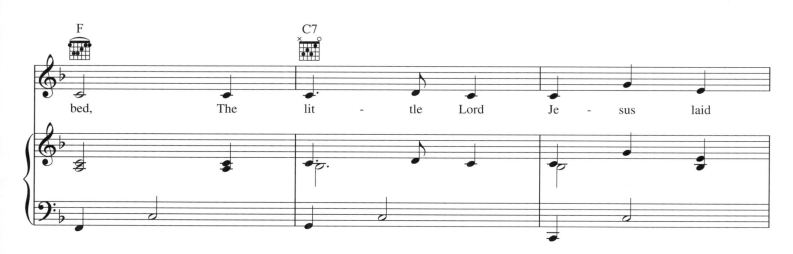

down His sweet head. The stars in the

sky _____ looked down where He lay, The

lit - tle Lord Je - sus, a - sleep on the

hay. The cat - tle are low - ing, the ba - by a -

AULD LANG SYNE

Words by ROBERT BURNS
Traditional Scottish Melody

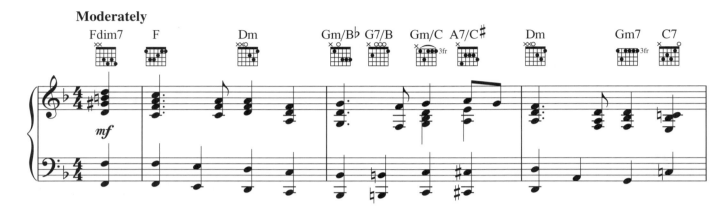

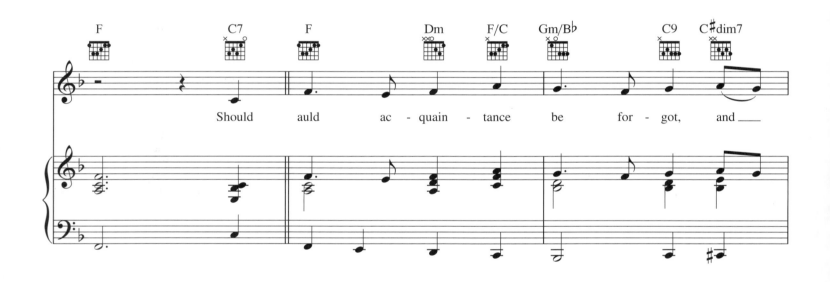

Should auld ac - quain - tance be for - got, and ___

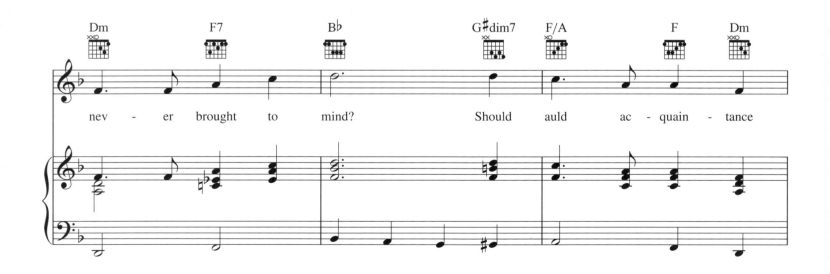

nev - er brought to mind? Should auld ac - quain - tance

BABY, IT'S COLD OUTSIDE

from the Motion Picture NEPTUNE'S DAUGHTER

By FRANK LOESSER

BECAUSE IT'S CHRISTMAS
(For All the Children)

Music by BARRY MANILOW
Lyric by BRUCE SUSSMAN and JACK FELDMAN

BRAZILIAN SLEIGH BELLS

By PERCY FAITH

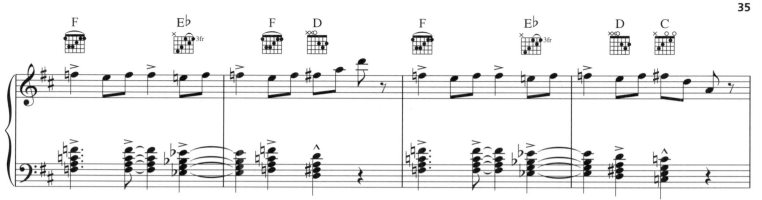

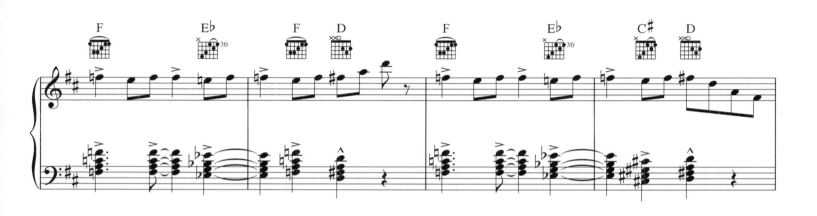

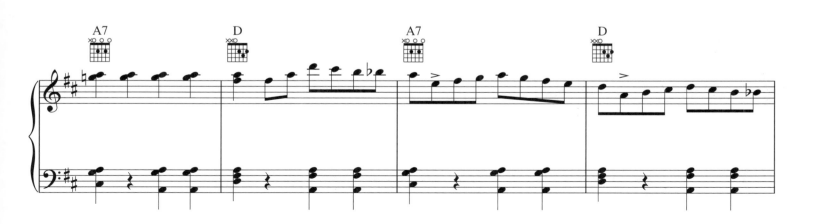

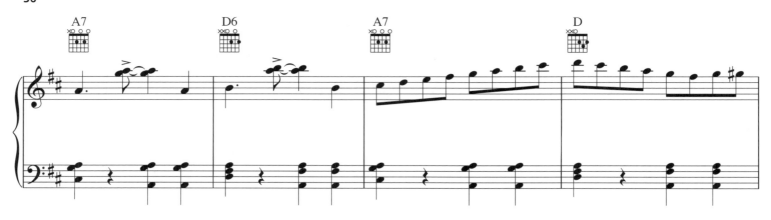

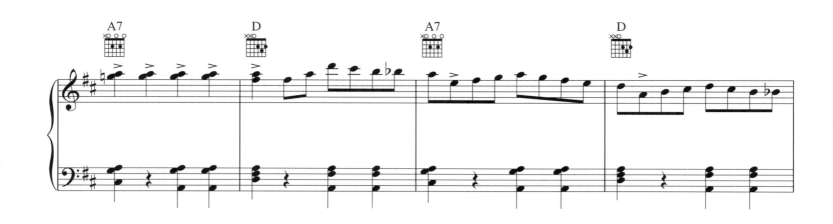

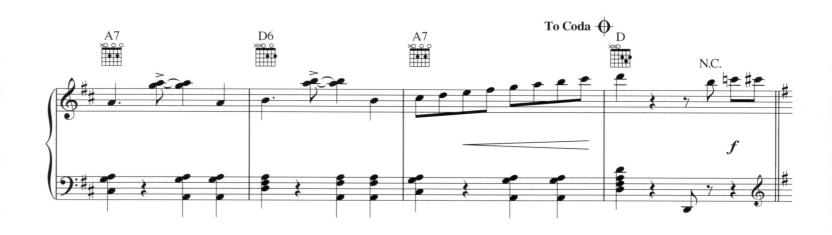

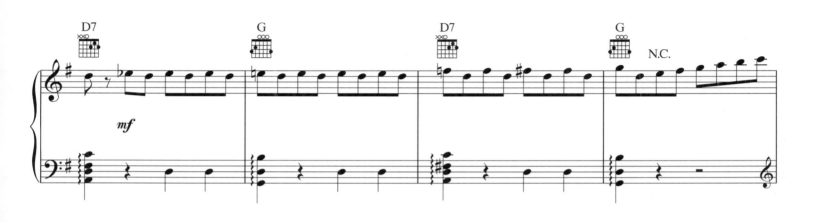

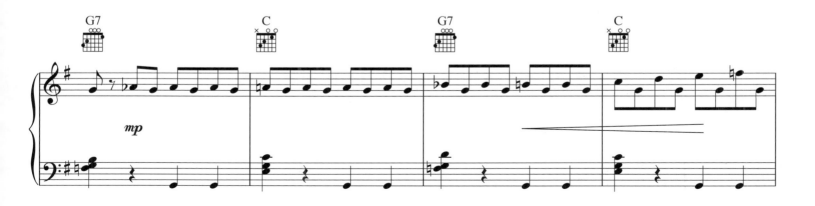

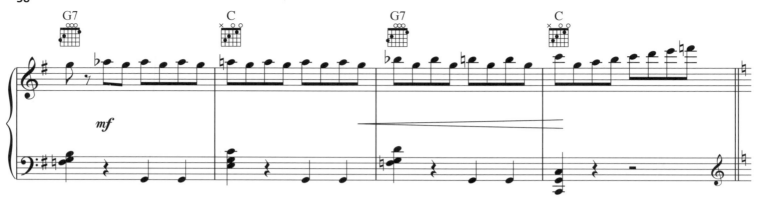

BLUE CHRISTMAS

Words and Music by BILLY HAYES
and JAY JOHNSON

Moderately

I'll have a blue Christ-mas, with-out you. _____ I'll be so

blue think-ing a-bout you. _____ Dec-o-ra-tions of

red on a green Christ-mas tree won't mean a thing if

CAROLING, CAROLING

Words by WIHLA HUTSON
Music by ALFRED BURT

THE CHIPMUNK SONG

Words and Music by
ROSS BAGDASARIAN

C-H-R-I-S-T-M-A-S

Words by JENNY LOU CARSON
Music by EDDY ARNOLD

Moderately

When I was but a young- ster, Christ- mas meant one

thing: that I'd be get- ting lots of toys that day. ____

____ I learned a whole lot dif- f'rent when Moth- er sat me

CHRISTMAS IS

Lyrics by SPENCE MAXWELL
Music by PERCY FAITH

Christ-mas is sleigh-bells, Christ-mas is shar-ing,

Christ-mas is hol-ly, Christ-mas is car-ing.

52

CHRISTMAS IS A-COMIN'
(May God Bless You)

Words and Music by
FRANK LUTHER

Moderately slow

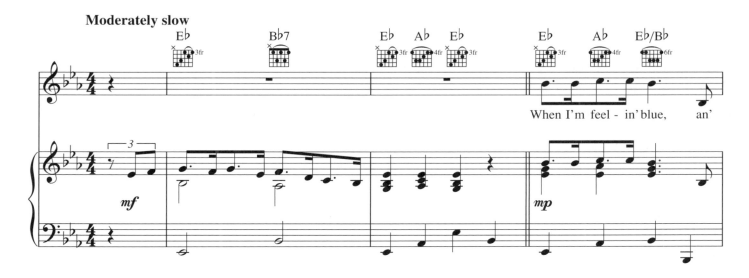

When I'm feel - in' blue, an'

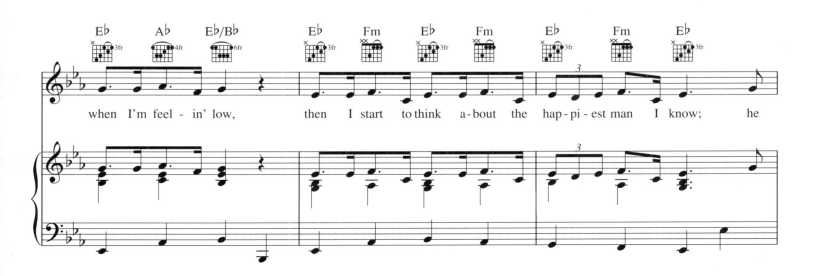

when I'm feel - in' low, then I start to think a-bout the hap-pi-est man I know; he

does-n't mind the snow an' he does-n't mind the rain, but all De-cem-ber you will hear him

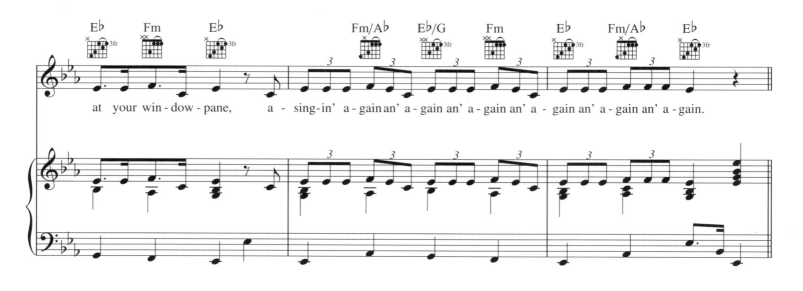

at your win-dow-pane, a - sing-in' a-gain an' a - gain an' a - gain an' a - gain an' a - gain an' a - gain.

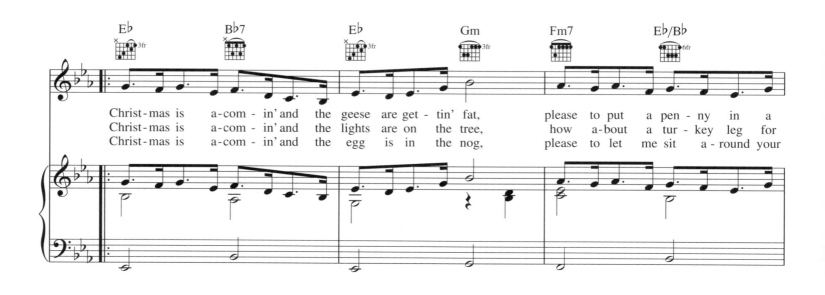

Christ-mas is a-com-in' and the geese are get-tin' fat, please to put a pen - ny in a
Christ-mas is a-com-in' and the lights are on the tree, how a-bout a tur-key leg for
Christ-mas is a-com-in' and the egg is in the nog, please to let me sit a-round your

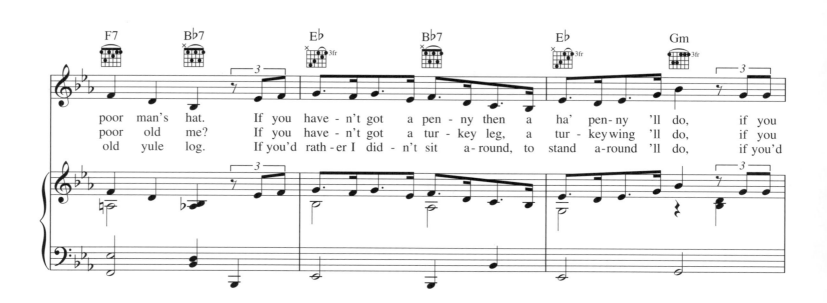

poor man's hat. If you have-n't got a pen-ny then a ha' pen-ny 'll do, if you
poor old me? If you have-n't got a tur-key leg, a tur-key wing 'll do, if you
old yule log. If you'd rath-er I did-n't sit a-round, to stand a-round 'll do, if you'd

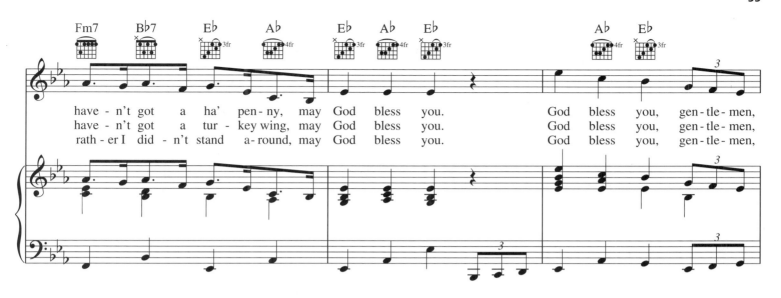

have-n't got a ha' pen-ny, may God bless you. God bless you, gen-tle-men,
have-n't got a tur-key wing, may God bless you. God bless you, gen-tle-men,
rath-er I did-n't stand a-round, may God bless you. God bless you, gen-tle-men,

God bless you, if you have-n't got a ha' pen-ny, may God bless you.
God bless you, if you have-n't got a tur-key wing, may God bless you.
God bless you, if you'd rath-er I did-n't stand a-round, may

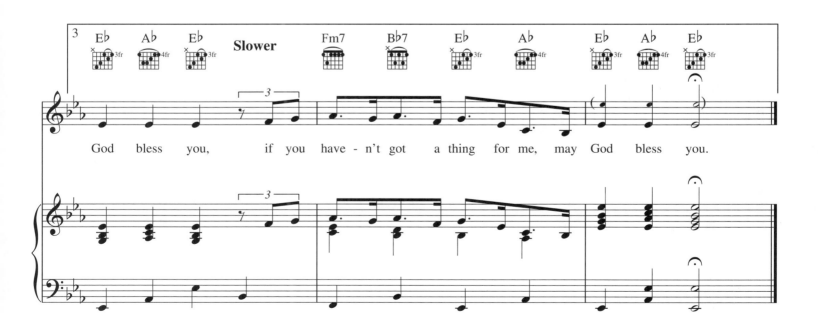

God bless you, if you have-n't got a thing for me, may God bless you.

THE CHRISTMAS SONG
(Chestnuts Roasting on an Open Fire)

Music and Lyric by MEL TORME
and ROBERT WELLS

CHRISTMAS TIME IS HERE

from A CHARLIE BROWN CHRISTMAS

Words by LEE MENDELSON
Music by VINCE GUARALDI

Christ - mas time is here, hap - pi - ness and
Snow - flakes in the air, car - ols ev - 'ry -

cheer. Fun for all that chil - dren call their
where. Old - en times and an - cient rhymes their of

fa - v'rite time of year.
love and dreams to share.

THE CHRISTMAS WALTZ

Words by SAMMY CAHN
Music by JULE STYNE

DO THEY KNOW IT'S CHRISTMAS?

Words and Music by M. URE
and B. GELDOF

DECK THE HALL

Traditional Welsh Carol

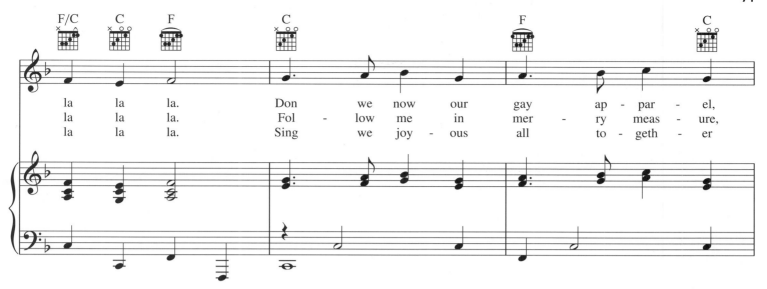

la la la la. Don we now our gay ap - par - el,
la la la la. Fol - low me in mer - ry meas - ure,
la la la la. Sing we joy - ous all to - geth - er

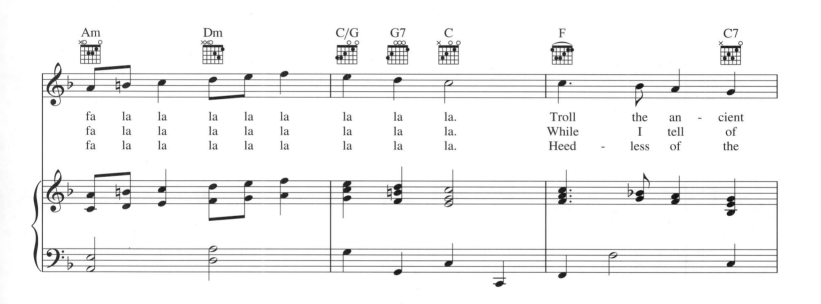

fa la la la la la la la la. Troll the an - cient
fa la la la la la la la la. While I tell of
fa la la la la la la la la. Heed - less of the

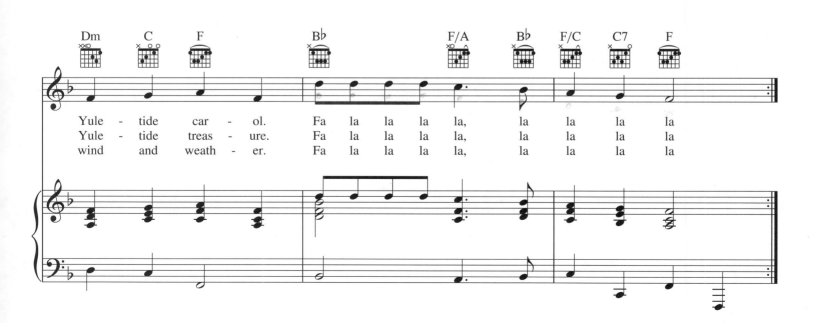

Yule - tide car - ol. Fa la la la la, la la la la
Yule - tide treas - ure. Fa la la la la, la la la la
wind and weath - er. Fa la la la la, la la la la

DO YOU HEAR WHAT I HEAR

Words and Music by NOEL REGNEY
and GLORIA SHAYNE

FELIZ NAVIDAD

Music and Lyrics by
JOSÉ FELICIANO

DON'T SAVE IT ALL FOR CHRISTMAS DAY

Words and Music by CELINE DION,
PETER ZIZZO and RIC WAKE

Don't get so bus-y that you miss

* Key of recording: Db

CODA

THE FIRST NOEL

17th Century English Carol
Music from W. Sandys' *Christmas Carols*

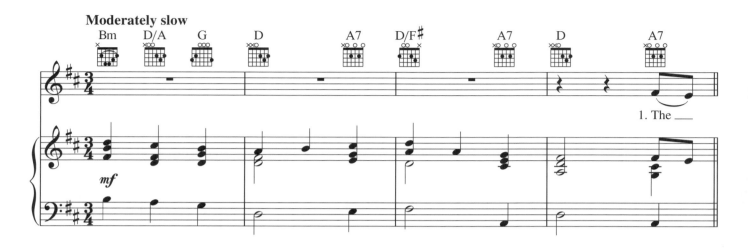

1. The __

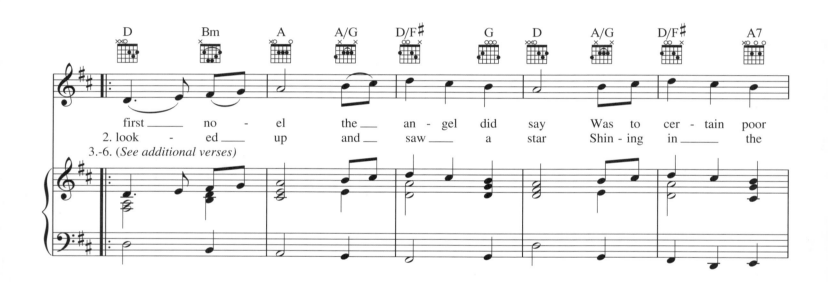

first __ no - el the __ an - gel did say Was to cer - tain poor
2. look - ed __ up and __ saw __ a star Shin - ing in __ the
3.-6. *(See additional verses)*

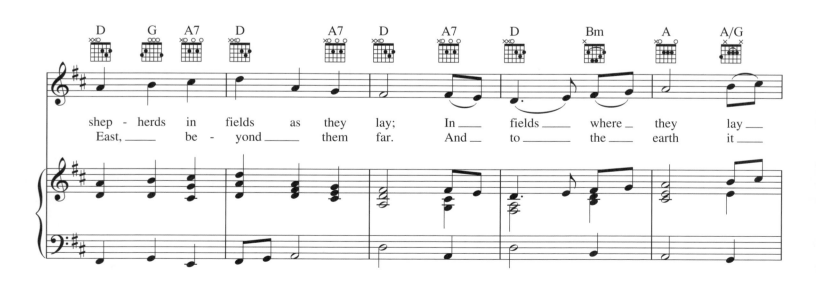

shep - herds in fields as they lay; In __ fields __ where they lay;
East, __ be - yond __ them far. And __ to __ the __ earth it __

Additional Verses

3. And by the light of that same star,
   Three wise men came from country far.
   To seek for a King was their intent,
   And to follow the star wherever it went.
   Refrain

4. This star drew nigh to the northwest;
   O'er Bethlehem it took its rest.
   And there it did both stop and stay,
   Right over the place where Jesus lay.
   Refrain

5. Then entered in those wise men three,
   Full rev'rently upon their knee;
   And offered there in His presence,
   Their gold and myrrh and frankincense.
   Refrain

6. Then let us all with one accord
   Sing praises to our heav'nly Lord,
   That hath made heav'n and earth of naught,
   And with His blood mankind hath bought.
   Refrain

FROSTY THE SNOW MAN

Words and Music by STEVE NELSON
and JACK ROLLINS

91

THE GIFT

Words and Music by TOM DOUGLAS
and JIM BRICKMAN

98

GOD REST YE MERRY, GENTLEMEN

19th Century English Carol

GRANDMA GOT RUN OVER BY A REINDEER

Words and Music by
RANDY BROOKS

You can say there's no such thing as San-ta, but as for me and Grand-pa, we be-

lieve.

Additional Lyrics

2. Now we're all so proud of Grandpa,
   He's been taking this so well.
   See him in there watching football,
   Drinking beer and playing cards with Cousin Mel.
   It's not Christmas without Grandma.
   All the family's dressed in black,
   And we just can't help but wonder:
   Should we open up her gifts or send them back?
   Chorus

3. Now the goose is on the table,
   And the pudding made of fig,
   And the blue and silver candles,
   That would just have matched the hair in Grandma's wig.
   I've warned all my friends and neighbors,
   Better watch out for yourselves.
   They should never give a license
   To a man who drives a sleigh and plays with elves.
   Chorus

THE GREATEST GIFT OF ALL

Words and Music by
JOHN JARVIS

GREENWILLOW CHRISTMAS
from GREENWILLOW

By FRANK LOESSER

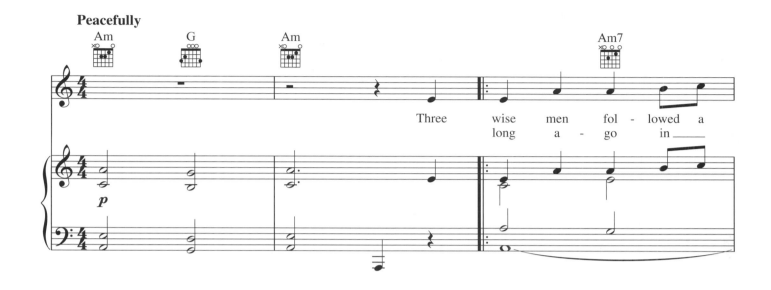

Three wise men fol-lowed a
long a - go in

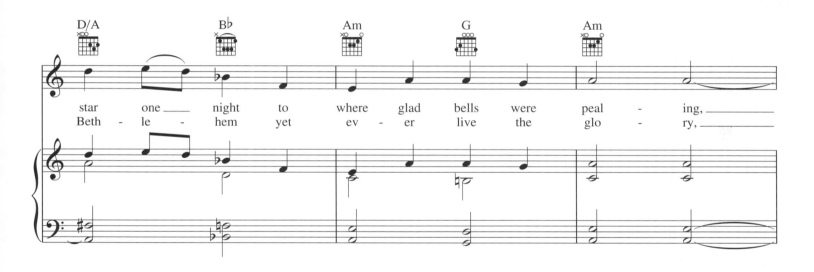

star one ___ night to where glad bells were peal - ing, ___
Beth - le - hem to yet ev - er live were the glo - ry, ___

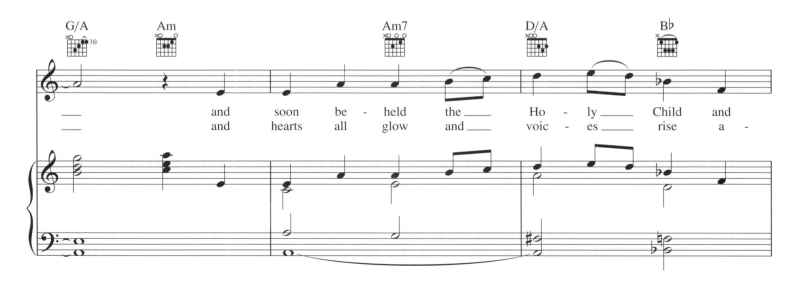

___ and soon be-held the ___ Ho - ly ___ Child and
___ and soon hearts all glow and ___ voic - es ___ rise a -

HAPPY CHRISTMAS, LITTLE FRIEND

Lyrics by OSCAR HAMMERSTEIN II
Music by RICHARD RODGERS

HAPPY HANUKKAH, MY FRIEND
(The Hanukkah Song)

Words and Music by JUSTIN WILDE
and DOUGLAS ALAN KONECKY

HAPPY HOLIDAY

from the Motion Picture Irving Berlin's HOLIDAY INN

Words and Music by
IRVING BERLIN

HE

Words by RICHARD MULLEN
Music by JACK RICHARDS

Moderately slow

mp

He can turn the tides and calm the an - gry
He can grant a wish or make a dream come

sea;
He a - lone de - cides who writes a
true,
He can paint the clouds and turn the

sym - pho - ny;
He lights ev - 'ry
gray to blue;
He a - lone knows

126

HAPPY XMAS
(War Is Over)

Words and Music by JOHN LENNON
and YOKO ONO

HARD CANDY CHRISTMAS
from THE BEST LITTLE WHOREHOUSE IN TEXAS

Words and Music by
CAROL HALL

HARK! THE HERALD ANGELS SING

Words by CHARLES WESLEY
Altered by GEORGE WHITEFIELD
Music by FELIX MENDELSSOHN-BARTHOLDY
Arranged by WILLIAM H. CUMMINGS

Hark! The her - ald an - gels sing, _____
Christ, by high - est heav'n a - dored, _____
Hail, the heav'n - born Prince of Peace! _____

"Glo - ry to the new - born King! Peace on earth, and
Christ, the ev - er - last - ing Lord; Late in time be -
Hail, the Sun of Right - eous - ness! Light and life to

mer - cy mild, _____ God and sin - ners rec - on - ciled."
hold Him come, _____ Off - spring of the vir - gin's womb.
all He brings, _____ Ris'n with heal - ing in His wings.

HERE COMES SANTA CLAUS
(Right Down Santa Claus Lane)

Words and Music by GENE AUTRY
and OAKLEY HALDEMAN

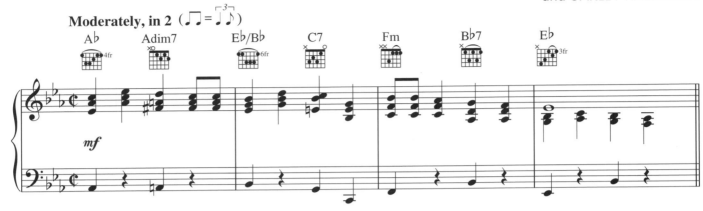

Here comes San-ta Claus! Here comes San-ta Claus! Right down San-ta Claus Lane!

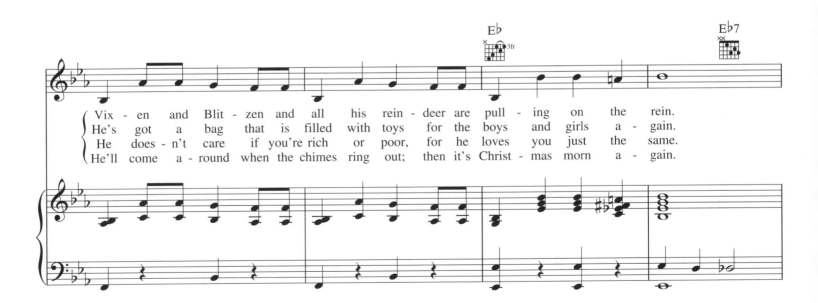

Vix-en and Blit-zen and all his rein-deer are pull-ing on the rein.
He's got a bag that is filled with toys for the boys and girls a-gain.
He does-n't care if you're rich or poor, for he loves you just the same.
He'll come a-round when the chimes ring out; then it's Christ-mas morn a-gain.

Bells are ring - ing, chil - dren sing - ing, all is mer - ry and
Hear those sleigh - bells jin - gle jan - gle, what a beau - ti - ful
San - ta knows that we're God's chil - dren; that makes ev - 'ry - thing
Peace on earth will come to all if we just fol - low the

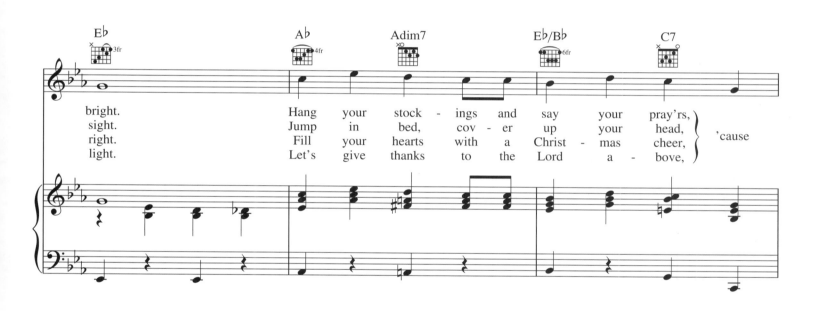

bright. Hang your stock - ings and say your pray'rs,
sight. Jump in bed, cov - er up your head, } 'cause
right. Fill your hearts with a Christ - mas cheer, }
light. Let's give thanks to the Lord a - bove, }

San - ta Claus comes to - night.   San - ta Claus comes to - night.

A HOLLY JOLLY CHRISTMAS

Music and Lyrics by
JOHNNY MARKS

(There's No Place Like)
HOME FOR THE HOLIDAYS

Words by AL STILLMAN
Music by ROBERT ALLEN

Moderately, with feeling

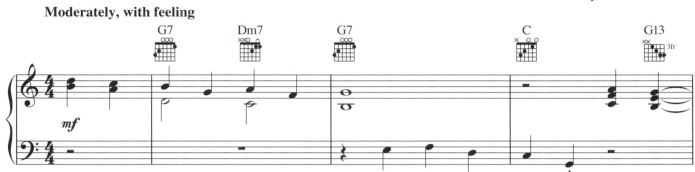

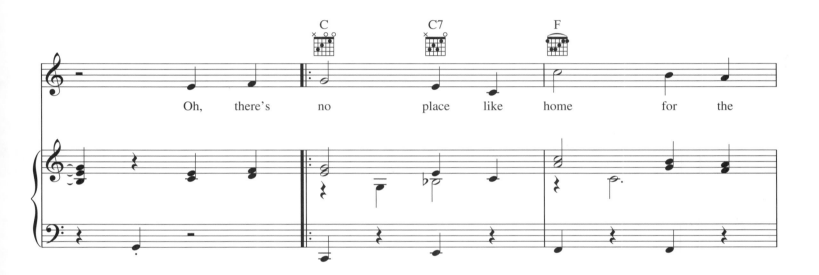

Oh, there's no place like home for the

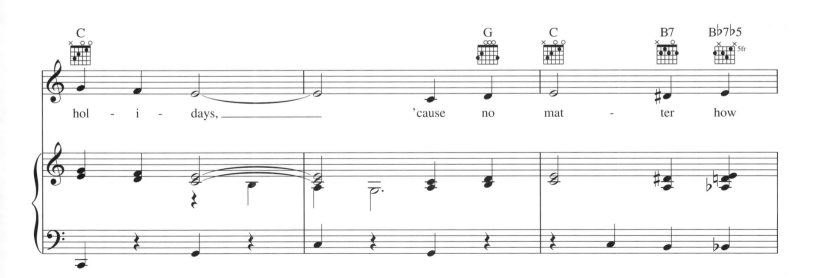

hol - i - days, _____ 'cause no mat - ter how

HYMNE

By VANGELIS

Slowly

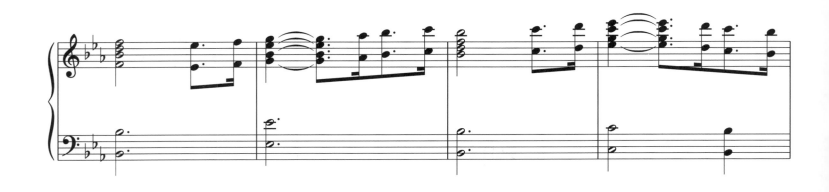

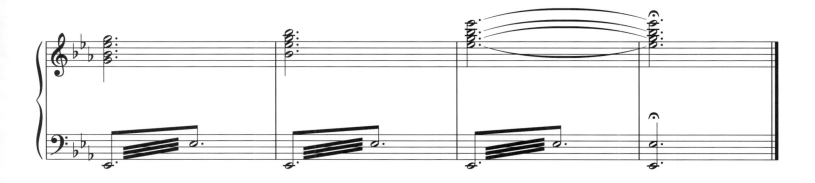

I HEARD THE BELLS ON CHRISTMAS DAY

Words by HENRY WADSWORTH LONGFELLOW
Adapted by JOHNNY MARKS
Music by JOHNNY MARKS

Moderately slow

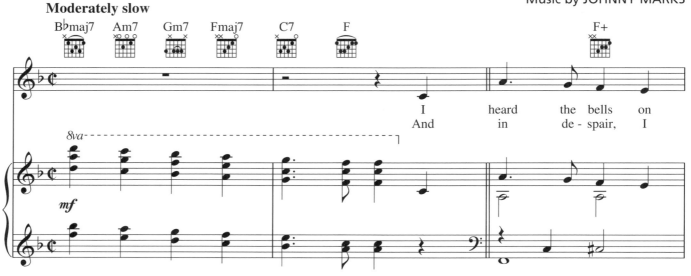

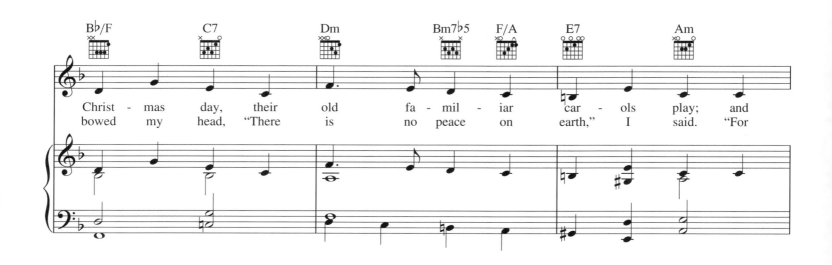

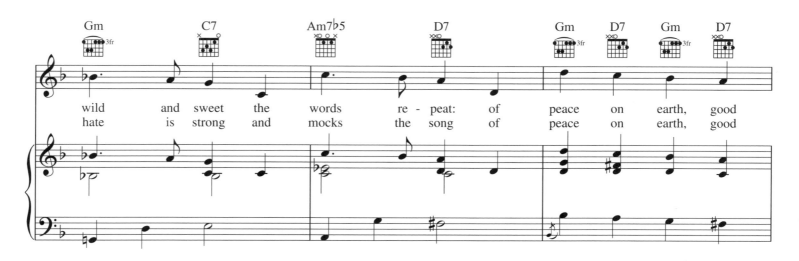

I SAW MOMMY KISSING SANTA CLAUS

Words and Music by
TOMMIE CONNOR

I'LL BE HOME FOR CHRISTMAS

Words and Music by KIM GANNON
and WALTER KENT

Lyrics:

I'm dream-ing to-night of a place I love, ___ e-ven more than I u-sual-ly do. And al-though I know it's a long road back, ___ I prom-ise you

I WONDER AS I WANDER

By JOHN JACOB NILES

I'VE GOT MY LOVE TO KEEP ME WARM

from the 20th Century Fox Motion Picture ON THE AVENUE

Words and Music by
IRVING BERLIN

IT CAME UPON THE MIDNIGHT CLEAR

Words by EDMUND HAMILTON SEARS
Music by RICHARD STORRS WILLIS

IT'S BEGINNING TO LOOK LIKE CHRISTMAS

By MEREDITH WILLSON

IT MUST HAVE BEEN THE MISTLETOE
(Our First Christmas)

By JUSTIN WILDE
and DOUG KONECKY

IT'S CHRISTMAS TIME ALL OVER THE WORLD

Words and Music by
HUGH MARTIN

Fast and happily

IT'S JUST ANOTHER
NEW YEAR'S EVE

Lyric by MARTY PANZER
Music by BARRY MANILOW

Slow Ballad

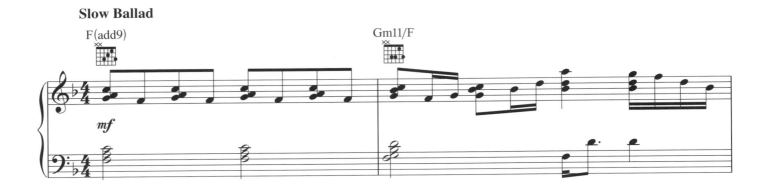

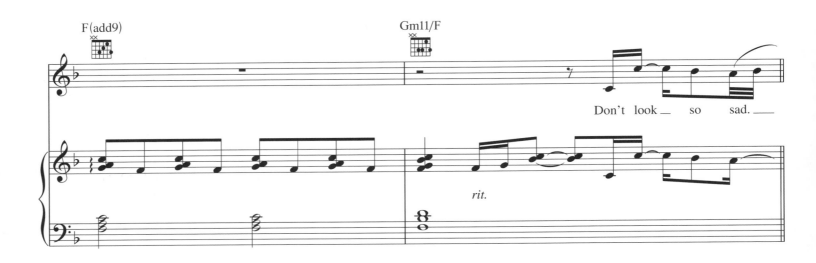

Don't look __ so sad. __

lone,

It's not __ so bad, __ you know. __
but we've __ made good __ friends, too. __
we've got __ the world, __ you know. __

It's just an-oth-er
Re-mem-ber all the
And it won't let us

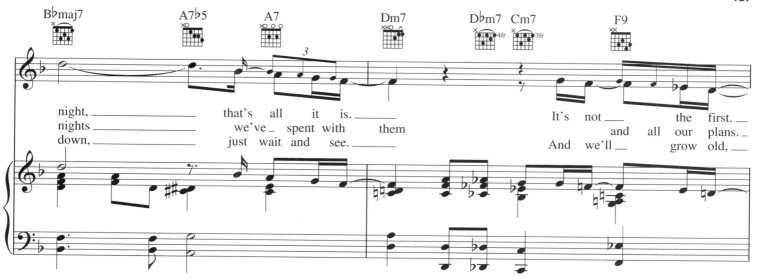

night, _____ that's all it is. _____ It's not _____ the first. _____
nights _____ we've_ spent with them and all our plans. _
down, _____ just wait and see. _____ And we'll_ grow old,

_____ It's not the worst, _ you know._ We've come through all _____
_____ Who says _____ they can't_ come true? _____ To - night's an - oth -
_____ but think _____ how wise_ we'll grow. _____ There's more, you know, _

_____ the rest. We'll get through this. _____ We've made_ mis - takes _

JINGLE-BELL ROCK

Words and Music by JOE BEAL
and JIM BOOTHE

JINGLE BELLS

Words and Music by
J. PIERPONT

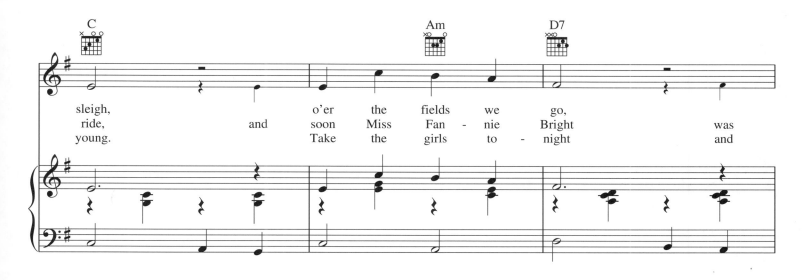

JOY TO THE WORLD

Words by ISAAC WATTS
Music by GEORGE FRIDERIC HANDEL
Arranged by LOWELL MASON

With spirit

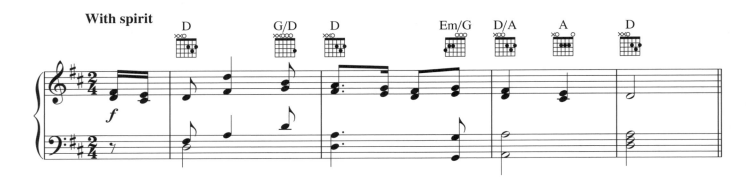

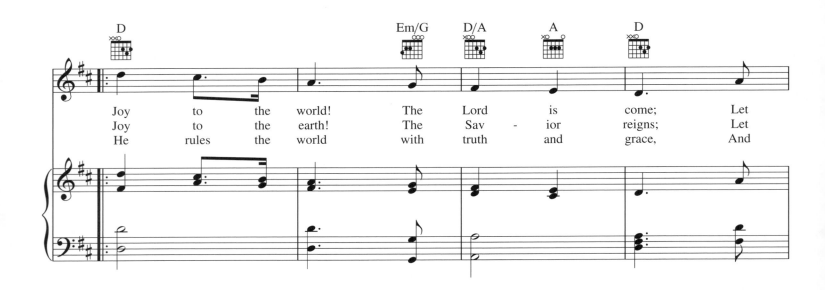

Joy to the world! The Lord is come; Let
Joy to the earth! The Sav - ior reigns; Let
He rules the world with truth and grace, And

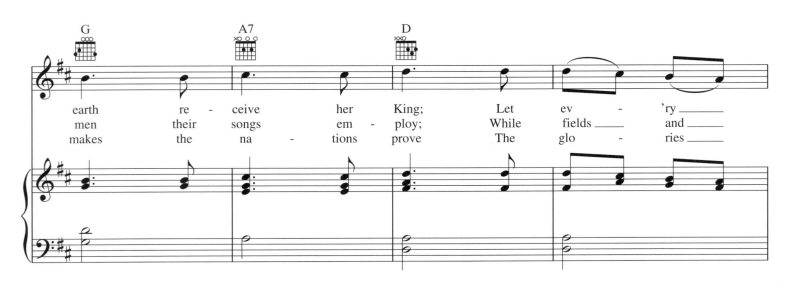

earth re - ceive her King; Let ev - 'ry _____ and _____
men their songs em - ploy; While fields _____ and _____
makes the na - tions prove The glo - ries _____

heart _____ pre - pare _____ Him _____ room, _____ and heav'n and na - ture _____
floods, _____ rocks, hills _____ and _____ plains _____ Re - peat the sound - ing _____
of _____ His right - eous - ness _____ And won - ders of His _____

sing, _____ And _____ heav'n and na - ture _____ sing, _____ And _____
joy, _____ Re - peat the sound - ing _____ joy, _____ Re -
love, _____ And _____ won - ders sound of His _____ love, _____ And _____

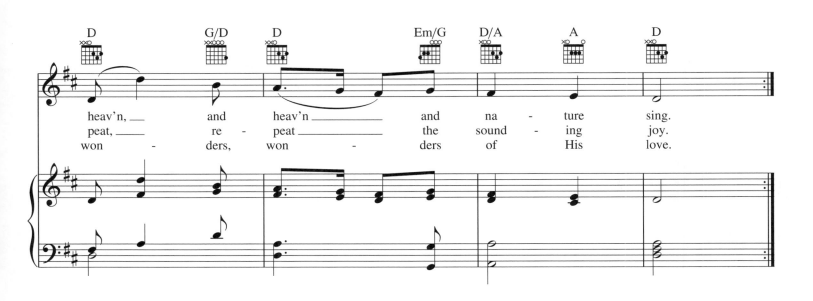

heav'n, _____ and heav'n _____ and na - ture sing.
peat, _____ re - peat _____ the sound - ing joy.
won - ders, won - ders sound of His love.

LAST CHRISTMAS

Words and Music by
GEORGE MICHAEL

THE LAST MONTH OF THE YEAR
(What Month Was Jesus Born In?)

Words and Music by VERA HALL
Adapted and Arranged by RUBY PICKENS TARTT
and ALAN LOMAX

LET IT SNOW! LET IT SNOW! LET IT SNOW!

Words by SAMMY CAHN
Music by JULE STYNE

LET'S HAVE AN OLD FASHIONED CHRISTMAS

Lyric by LARRY CONLEY
Music by JOE SOLOMON

(Everybody's Waitin' For)
THE MAN WITH THE BAG

Words and Music by HAROLD STANLEY,
IRVING TAYLOR and DUDLEY BROOKS

LITTLE SAINT NICK

Words and Music by BRIAN WILSON
and MIKE LOVE

Recorded a half step lower.

A MARSHMALLOW WORLD

Words by CARL SIGMAN
Music by PETER DE ROSE

It's a marsh-mal-low world in the win-ter _____ when the
snow comes to cov-er the ground. It's the time for play. ___ It's a
whipped-cream day. ___ I wait for it the whole year 'round. Those are

MELE KALIKIMAKA

Words and Music by
ALEX ANDERSON

MERRY CHRISTMAS, DARLING

Words and Music by RICHARD CARPENTER
and FRANK POOLER

Greet- ing cards have all been sent, the Christ- mas rush is through,

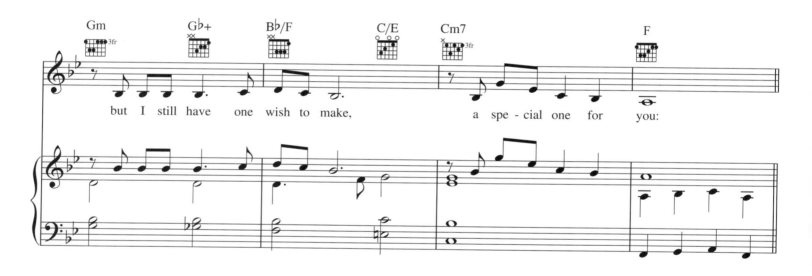

but I still have one wish to make, a spe- cial one for you:

Mer- ry Christ- mas, dar- ling. We're a- part, that's true; but

THE MERRY CHRISTMAS POLKA

Words by PAUL FRANCIS WEBSTER
Music by SONNY BURKE

Moderate Polka tempo

They're

tun- ing up the fid- dles now, the fid- dles now, the fid- dles now. There's

wine to warm the mid- dles now and set your head a- whirl. A-

MERRY CHRISTMAS, BABY

Words and Music by LOU BAXTER
and JOHNNY MOORE

D.S. al Coda

Solo ends Well, I'm

CODA

I said mer -

- ry Christ-mas, ba - by,

yes, you sure did   treat me nice.

Mer - ry,

MISTER SANTA

Words and Music by
PAT BALLARD

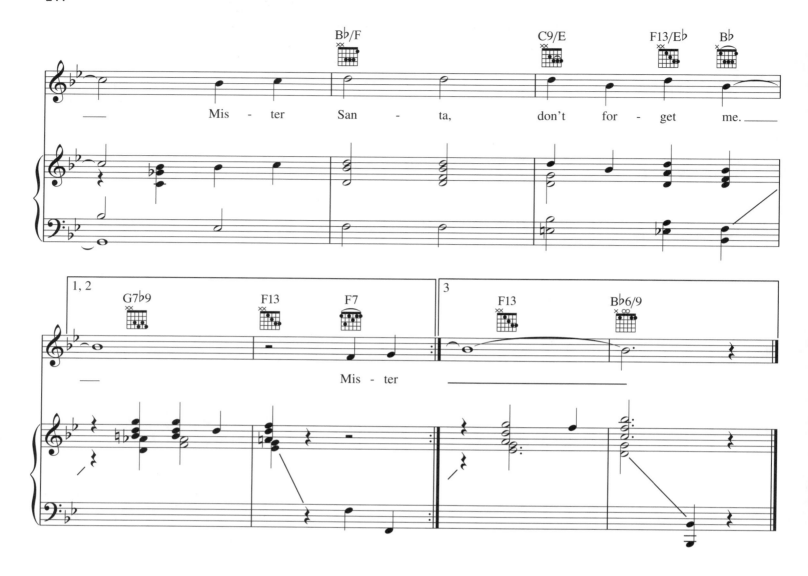

Additional Lyrics

2. Mister Santa, dear old Saint Nick,
   Be awful careful and please don't get sick.
   Put on your coat when breezes are blowin',
   And when you cross the street look where you're goin'.
   Santa, we (I) love you so,
   We (I) hope you never get lost in the snow.
   Take your time when you unpack,
   Mister Santa, don't hurry back.

3. Mister Santa, we've been so good;
   We've washed the dishes and done what we should.
   Made up the beds and scrubbed up our toesies,
   We've used a kleenex when we've blown our nosesies.
   Santa, look at our ears, they're clean as whistles,
   We're sharper than shears.
   Now we've put you on the spot,
   Mister Santa, bring us a lot.

THE NIGHT BEFORE CHRISTMAS SONG

Music by JOHNNY MARKS
Lyrics adapted by JOHNNY MARKS
from CLEMENT MOORE'S Poem

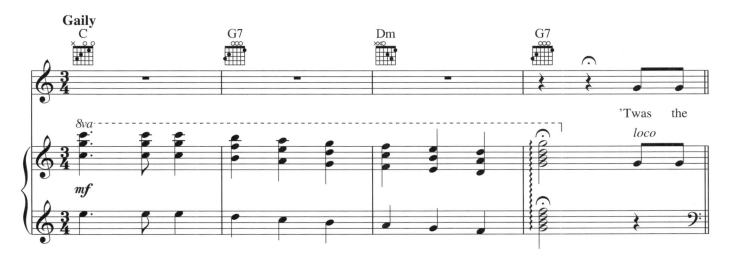

night be-fore Christ-mas and all through the house, not a crea-ture was
up to the house-top the rein-deer soon flew, with the sleigh full of

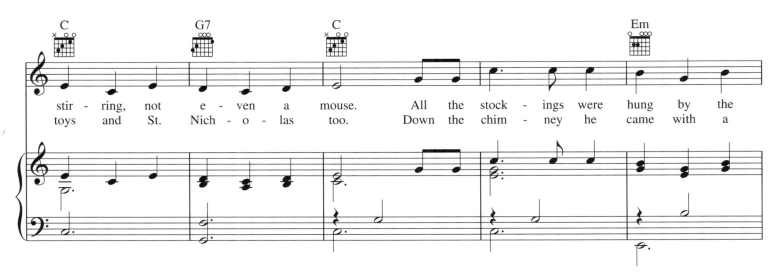

stir-ring, not e-ven a mouse. All the stock-ings were hung by the
toys and St. Nich-o-las too. Down the chim-ney he came with a

MISTLETOE AND HOLLY

Words and Music by FRANK SINATRA,
DOK STANFORD and HENRY W. SANICOLA

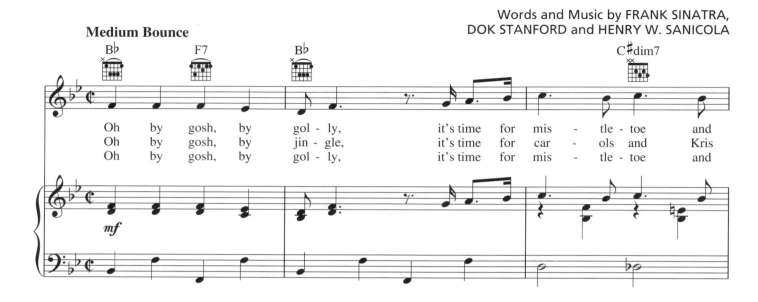

Oh by gosh, by gol - ly, it's time for mis - tle - toe and
Oh by gosh, by jin - gle, it's time for car - ols and Kris
Oh by gosh, by gol - ly, it's time for mis - tle - toe and

hol - ly. _____ Tast - y pheas - ants, Christ - mas pres - ents,
Krin - gle. _____ O - ver - eat - ing, mer - ry greet - ings,
hol - ly. _____ Fan - cy ties an' gran - ny's pies an'

coun - try - sides cov - ered with snow.
from _____ rel - a - tives you don't know.

Then comes that big night, __ giv-ing the tree the trim,

you'll hear voic-es by star-light __ sing-ing a yule-tide hymn.

D.C. al Coda

CODA folks steal-in' a kiss or two as they whis-per, "Mer-ry

Christ-mas to you." _____

THE MOST WONDERFUL DAY OF THE YEAR

Music and Lyrics by
JOHNNY MARKS

THE MOST WONDERFUL TIME OF THE YEAR

Words and Music by EDDIE POLA
and GEORGE WYLE

MY FAVORITE THINGS
from THE SOUND OF MUSIC

Lyrics by OSCAR HAMMERSTEIN II
Music by RICHARD RODGERS

MY ONLY WISH THIS YEAR

Words and Music by BRIAN KIERULF
and JOSHUA SCHWARTZ

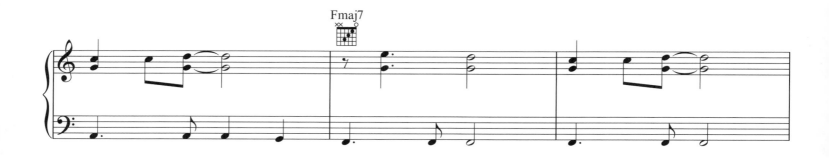

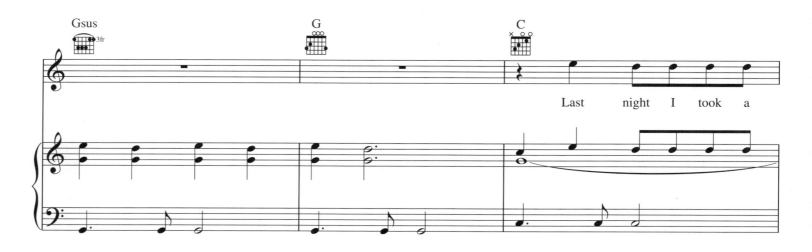

Last night I took a

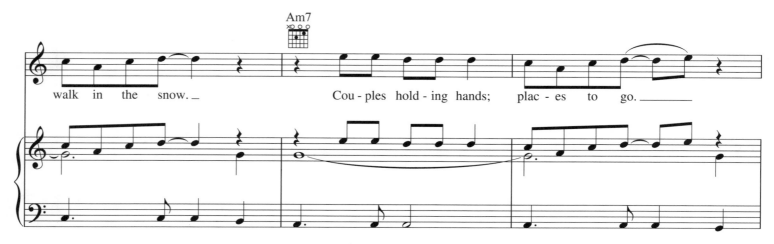

walk in the snow. _____ Cou-ples hold-ing hands; plac-es to go. _____

NUTTIN' FOR CHRISTMAS

Words and Music by ROY BENNETT
and SID TEPPER

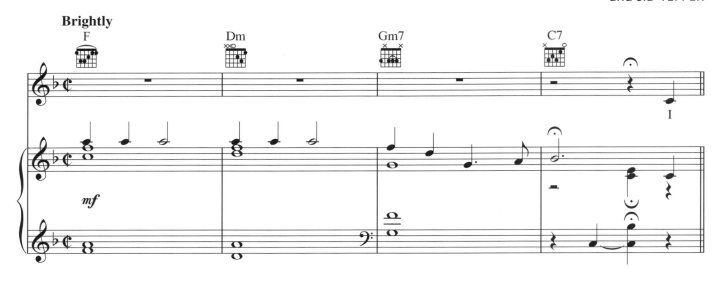

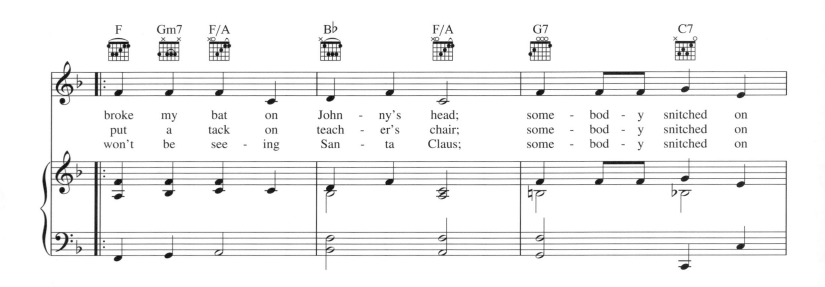

broke   my   bat   on   John - ny's   head;   some - bod - y   snitched   on
put   a   tack   on   teach - er's   chair;   some - bod - y   snitched   on
won't   be   see - ing   San - ta   Claus;   some - bod - y   snitched   on

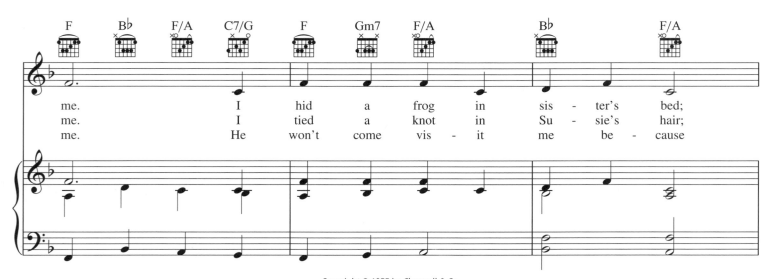

me.   I   hid   a   frog   in   sis - ter's   bed;
me.   I   tied   a   knot   in   Su - sie's   hair;
me.   He   won't   come   vis - it   me   be - cause

O CHRISTMAS TREE

Traditional German Carol

O Christ - mas tree! O Christ - mas tree, you
Christ - mas tree! O Christ - mas tree, much
Christ - mas tree! O Christ - mas tree, thy

stand in ver - dant beau - ty! O Christ - mas tree, O
pleas - ure doth thou bring me! O Christ - mas tree, O
can - dles shine out bright - ly! O Christ - mas tree, O

Christ - mas tree, you stand in ver - dant beau - ty! Your
Christ - mas tree, much pleas - ure doth thou bring me! For
Christ - mas tree, thy can - dles shine out bright - ly! Each

O COME, ALL YE FAITHFUL
(Adeste Fideles)

Words and Music by JOHN FRANCIS WADE
Latin Words translated by FREDERICK OAKELEY

O HOLY NIGHT

French Words by PLACIDE CAPPEAU
English Words by JOHN S. DWIGHT
Music by ADOLPHE ADAM

O ho - ly night,_____ the
Tru - ly He taught us to

stars are bright - ly shin - ing; it is the night of the
love one an - oth - er; His law is love, and His

dear Sav - ior's birth._____ Long lay the
gos - pel is peace._____ Chains shall He

O LITTLE TOWN OF BETHLEHEM

Words by PHILLIPS BROOKS
Music by LEWIS H. REDNER

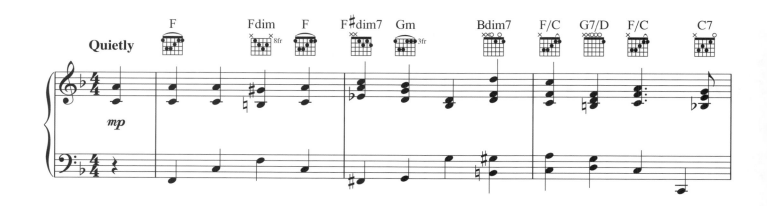

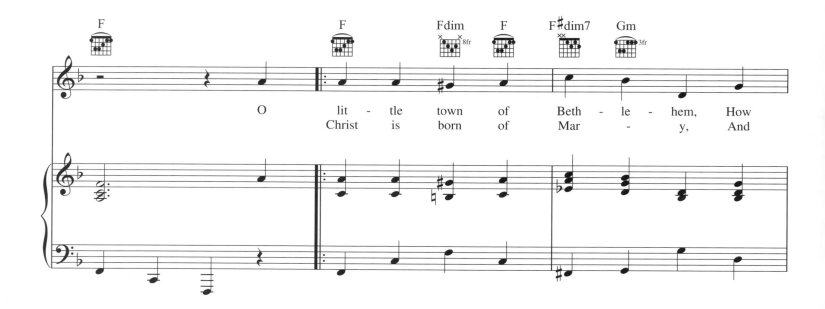

O lit - tle town of Beth - le - hem, How
Christ is born of Mar - y, And

still we ___ see thee lie! A - bove thy deep and
gath - ered ___ all a - bove, While mor - tals sleep the

OLD TOY TRAINS

Words and Music by
ROGER MILLER

PRETTY PAPER

Words and Music by
WILLIE NELSON

Slowly, with expression

Crow-ded streets, bus-y feet hus-tle by him. _____ Down-town shop-pers, Christ-mas is nigh. _____ There he sits all a-lone on the side-walk, _____ hop-ing _____ that you won't pass him

ROCKIN' AROUND THE CHRISTMAS TREE

Music and Lyrics by
JOHNNY MARKS

SANTA CLAUS IS COMIN' TO TOWN

Words by HAVEN GILLESPIE
Music by J. FRED COOTS

RUDOLPH THE RED-NOSED REINDEER

Music and Lyrics by
JOHNNY MARKS

SANTA BABY

By JOAN JAVITS,
PHIL SPRINGER and TONY SPRINGER

SANTA, BRING MY BABY BACK
(To Me)

Words and Music by CLAUDE DeMETRUIS
and AARON SCHROEDER

SHAKE ME I RATTLE
(Squeeze Me I Cry)

Words and Music by HAL HACKADY
and CHARLES NAYLOR

SILENT NIGHT

Words by JOSEPH MOHR
Translated by JOHN F. YOUNG
Music by FRANZ X. GRUBER

Quietly

Si - lent night,
Si - lent night,
Si - lent night,

ho - ly night! All is calm,
ho - ly night! Shep - herds quake
ho - ly night! Son of God,

all is bright. Round yon Vir - gin
at the sight. Glo - ries stream from
love's pure light. Ra - diant beams from

SILVER AND GOLD

Music and Lyrics by
JOHNNY MARKS

SILVER BELLS

from the Paramount Picture THE LEMON DROP KID

Words and Music by JAY LIVINGSTON
and RAY EVANS

SNOWFALL

Lyrics by RUTH THORNHILL
Music by CLAUDE THORNHILL

SOMEWHERE IN MY MEMORY

from the Twentieth Century Fox Motion Picture HOME ALONE

Words by LESLIE BRICUSSE
Music by JOHN WILLIAMS

SPECIAL GIFT

Words and Music by MYRON DAVIS
and STANLEY BROWN

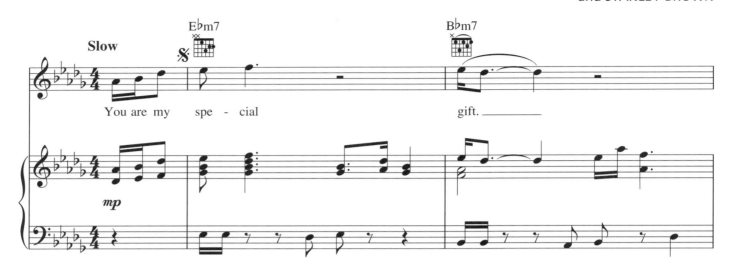

You are my spe - cial gift. _____

I have searched ev-'ry-where; noth-ing else can com-pare. Gift. _ You are my

spe - cial gift. _____

THE STAR CAROL

Lyric by WIHLA HUTSON
Music by ALFRED BURT

Tenderly, with much expression

Long years a - go on a deep_ win - ter night, High in the
Je - sus, the Lord was that Ba - by so small, Laid down to
Dear Ba - by Je - sus, how ti - ny Thou art, I'll make a

heav'ns a____ star____ shone bright, While in a man - ger a
sleep in a hum - ble stall; Then came the star and it
place for___ Thee_ in my heart, And when the stars in the

wee in - fant lay, Sweet - ly a - sleep on a bed of hay.
stood o - ver - head, Shed - ding its light 'round His lit - tle bed.
heav - ens I see, Ev - er and al - ways I think of Thee.

SUZY SNOWFLAKE

Words and Music by SID TEPPER
and ROY BENNETT

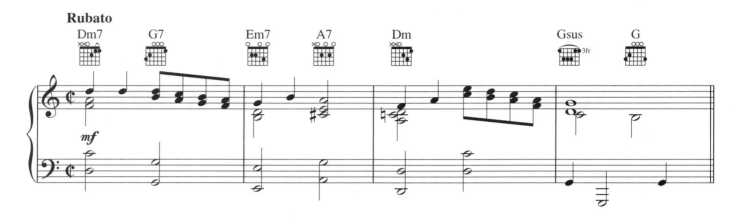

Here comes Su-zy Snow-flake, dressed in a snow-white
Here comes Su-zy Snow-flake, soon you will hear her

gown, tap, tap, tap-pin' at your win-dow-pane to
say: "Come out, ev-'ry-one, and play with me; I

TENNESSEE CHRISTMAS

Words and Music by AMY GRANT
and GARY CHAPMAN

Moderate 4

Come on weath-er-man __ give us __ a fore-
Ev-'ry now __ and then __ I get __ a wan-

-cast snow-y white. __
-derin' urge __ to see, __

Can't you hear __ the prayers __ of ev-'ry child-
may-be Cal-i-for-nia, may-be Tin-

THAT CHRISTMAS FEELING

Words and Music by BENNIE BENJAMIN
and GEORGE WEISS

THE TWELVE DAYS OF CHRISTMAS

Traditional English Carol

THIS CHRISTMAS

Words and Music by DONNY HATHAWAY
and NADINE McKINNOR

WE WISH YOU A MERRY CHRISTMAS

Traditional English Folksong

WHAT ARE YOU DOING NEW YEAR'S EVE?

By FRANK LOESSER

May-be it's much too ear-ly in the game, __ Ah, but I thought I'd

ask you just the same, __ what are you do-ing new year's,

New Year's Eve? Won-der whose arms will

WHEN SANTA CLAUS GETS YOUR LETTER

Music and Lyrics by
JOHNNY MARKS

359

THE WHITE WORLD OF WINTER

Words by MITCHELL PARISH
Music by HOAGY CARMICHAEL

WONDERFUL CHRISTMASTIME

Words and Music by
McCARTNEY

YOU DON'T HAVE TO BE ALONE

Words and Music by VEIT RENN,
JOSHUA CHASEZ and DAVID NICOLL

Slowly

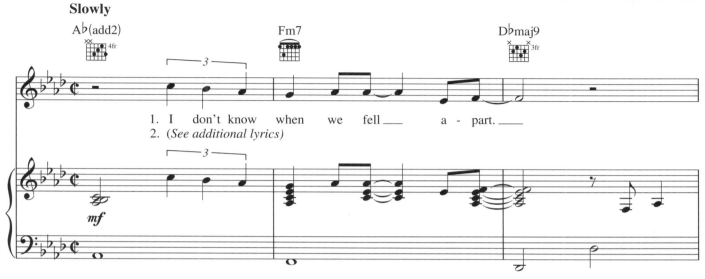

1. I don't know when we fell ___ a - part. ___
2. (See additional lyrics)

The love that we had was like ___ a work ___ of art. ___

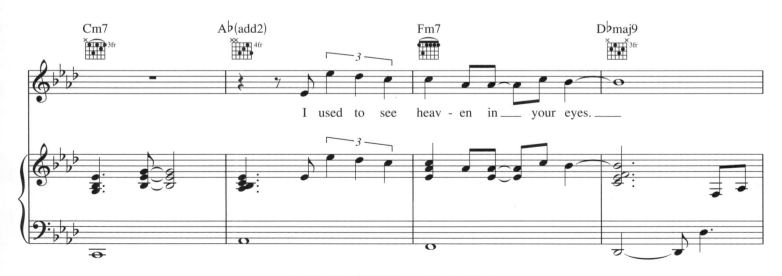

I used to see heav - en in ___ your eyes. ___

Additional Lyrics

2. And I had only one wish on my list.
For me, you would be the perfect gift.
There's nothing colder than an empty home.
And hotter days were never meant to be alone.
The smiles we gave when our hearts were safe
By each other's love and warmth.
That subsided now, no happiness around.
If I can only find a way to your heart.
Chorus:

YOU'RE ALL I WANT FOR CHRISTMAS

Words and Music by GLEN MOORE
and SEGER ELLIS